DATE DUE		
AP 22 '99		
MY 06 '99		
MY 19 '99		
JE 23 '99		
AG 03 '99		
FE 23 '00		

ANIMAL CRAFTS

By Iain MacLeod-Brudenell
Photographs by Zul Mukhida

Contents

Gareth Stevens Publishing
MILWAUKEE

About this book

What's your favorite animal? Perhaps it's your pet, or maybe it's a wild animal that you've seen only in books or on television. This book is about real and imaginary animals. It shows you how to make craft projects based on animals and gives plenty of ideas to help you design your own.

This book will tell you about stories, traditions, and crafts from around the world that are based on animals. Try to find out more about these animals and crafts. You will find information about places to visit and books to read at the back of the book.

Some of the craft activities in this book are more complicated than others and will take longer to finish. It might be fun to ask some friends to help with these activities, such as making the lion mask on page 6.

Before you start working on any of the craft projects, read through the instructions carefully. Most of the step-by-step instructions have a number. Look for the same number in the picture to see what each stage of your project should look like.

Before you begin

Collect everything listed in the "You will need" box or general project directions.

Ask an adult's permission if you are going to use a sharp tool, dye cloth, or use an oven.

Prepare a clear work surface.

If the activity is going to be messy, cover the surface with old newspaper or a waterproof sheet.

3

Animal people

In many stories, animals are main characters. They are given human qualities, such as being honest or greedy. In Aesop's fables, talking animals are used to show human faults. Do you think animals and people have similar characteristics?

"Puss in Boots" is the story of a very clever cat that wears long boots. After many adventures, Puss in Boots makes his master rich and powerful. Today, this story is often retold in pantomime.

Try making a glove puppet of Puss in Boots

> **You will need:**
> - felt
> - white glue
> - a pin
> - paints
> - paintbrushes
> - a large needle
> - thread
> - scissors
> - braid or scraps of material
> - self-hardening clay or salt dough (see page 30)

1 Cut out two tunic shapes from felt. Glue or sew the side seams of the tunic together. The tunic must be big enough for your hand to fit inside. Decorate with braid or scraps of material.

2 Cut out two rectangles of felt for the legs. On each rectangle, glue or sew the long edges together. Glue or stitch the legs to the inside of the front of the tunic.

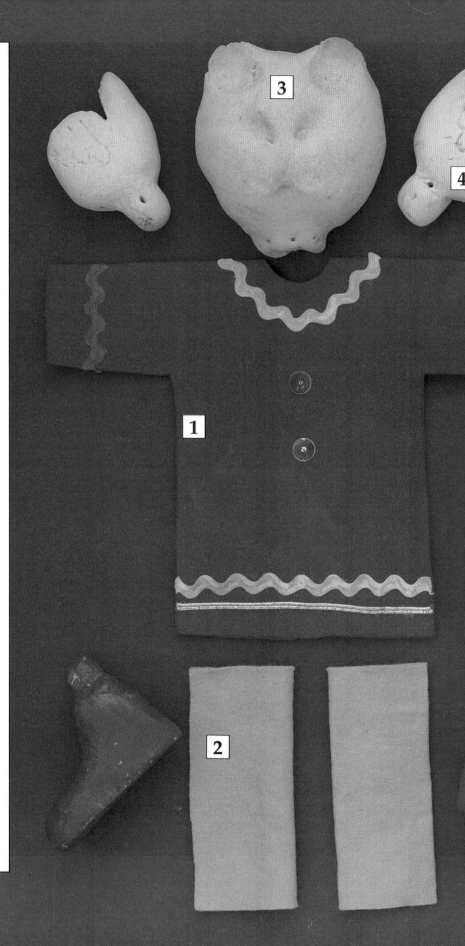

3 Make the head from a ball of clay or salt dough. Use the tip of one finger to make the head hollow. Squeeze the bottom of the head into a neck, which will fit into the neck of the tunic.

Make about eight holes around the edge of the neck with a pin. The holes should be big enough for a large needle and thread to pass through. Let the clay dry, or bake the salt dough. Then paint the head.

4 Make two paws and two boots from the clay or dough. Pinch the ends as shown. Make one hole that runs through each end. Then make another hole, so that the holes are at quarter turns. Let the clay dry, or bake the dough. Then paint the paws and boots.

5 To join the head to the tunic, stitch through the neck of the tunic and then through a hole in the puppet's neck. Continue until you have stitched all the way around. Stitch the boots to the legs and then stitch the paws to the arms of the tunic in the same way.

Put your glove puppet on your hand and make Puss in Boots move. Try to make puppets of other animal characters and put on a puppet show.

5

Lion tales

In many African countries, the lion is considered such a brave and dignified animal it is known as "king of the beasts."

Try making a lion mask

You will need:
- masking tape or a stapler
- newspaper torn into strips
- wallpaper paste without fungicide
- scraps of paper and material for decoration
- cardboard
- scissors
- egg cartons
- paints
- paintbrushes
- white glue
- felt

1 Cut the cardboard into long strips about 2 inches (5 centimeters) wide. You might use the cardboard from an old box. Make a hoop that is big enough to go over your head and rest on your shoulders. Fasten the cardboard strip into a hoop with tape or a stapler.

Use the hoop as the base for a cardboard cage. Fasten a number of strips that fit over your head from one side of the base to the other, as shown.

Cover the cage with a layer of strips of torn newspaper that have been dipped into wallpaper paste. When the cage is covered with this papier-mâché, let it dry. Then paste another layer on top. Cover with about four layers of papier-mâché. Let it dry.

2 Put the cage over your head and feel where you should make the holes for the lion's eyes and nostrils. Take the mask off and cut out the eye and nostril holes. Make the lion's features with crumpled paper and egg cartons, and glue onto the mask. Cover the mask with another layer of papier-mâché. Let it dry.

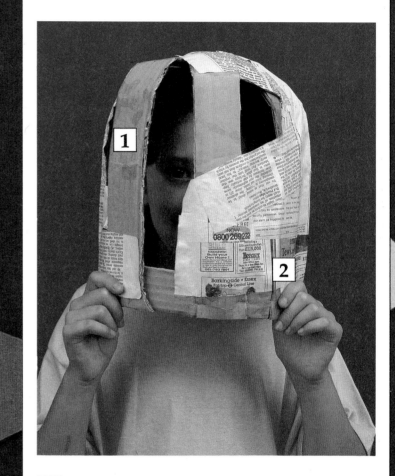

3 Paint the mask. You can use colored felt to make a mane.

Mythical creatures

Hundreds of years ago, sailors were often the only people to travel great distances. On their return home, they told stories of strange and wonderful creatures they had seen. Artists listened to the sailors' descriptions and made drawings of the creatures. Sometimes the drawings were accurate, but sometimes the creatures looked magical and amazing.

Many creatures and monsters in legends and myths are a combination of two animals or part of an animal and part of a person. A centaur is a mythical creature that is half-horse and half-human. A mermaid is a creature that is half-woman and half-fish. The griffin is a monster that is a combination of two animals. An ancient story says that the griffin is the offspring of a lion and an eagle. The griffin kept guard over hidden treasures.

Try making your own paper creatures that are a mixture of animal parts or a mixture of animals and people.

You will need:	
• a pencil	• a knitting needle
• scissors	or hole puncher
• colored cardboard	• white glue
• paper fasteners	• Popsicle sticks

Before you start, it might help to look at photographs of different kinds of animals, such as wild and farm animals. Look at the shapes of their heads, legs, arms, paws, beaks, and wings.

1 Choose one animal and draw the outline of its head, body, arms, and legs separately on colored cardboard. Cut these pieces out carefully.

2 Make holes at the joints with a hole puncher or a knitting needle. Don't make the holes too near the edge of the paper because it might tear.

3 Use paper fasteners to join the parts together.

4 Make parts for lots of different kinds of animals. How many creatures can you make? Try making a mermaid or a centaur. Where will your creature live?

To make a creature into a shadow puppet, glue or tape Popsicle sticks to the back of the head and the elbows or wrists. Let the legs dangle. Stand in front of a well-lit wall, move the sticks, and see the shadow of the creature move.

Dragon fire

According to legend, dragons lived in many parts of the world. In Japanese and Chinese legends, dragons are friendly and help to keep order. But in European legends, they are often cruel and cunning.

Look for dragons on flags and statues.

Try making a flying dragon

You will need:
- colored paper or thin cardboard
- scissors
- a pencil
- a hole puncher or knitting needle
- two paper fasteners
- a 10-inch (25-cm) piece of thin dowel
- three thin pieces of coated wire about 18 inches (45 cm) each in length

1 To help you draw the dragon's shape, look at pictures of dragons in books. Draw and cut out a paper dragon's body with a head and tail.

2 Draw and cut out four separate legs. Use a hole puncher or knitting needle to make two holes in each leg — one at the foot and the other near the top, as shown.

3 Make one hole at the back of the body for the back legs and one hole at the front of the body for the front legs.

4 Join two legs to the front of the body with a paper fastener, as shown. Then join the two back legs to the body in the same way.

5 Draw and cut out two wings. Make a hole near the outer tip of each wing, as shown. Make tabs by folding back 3/8 inch (1 cm) of paper at the base of the wings.

6 Take one wing and glue or tape the tab to the body. Attach the other wing to the other side of the dragon's body in the same way.

7 Make holes for the dowel in the body — one near the top in the middle and the other at the bottom in the middle.

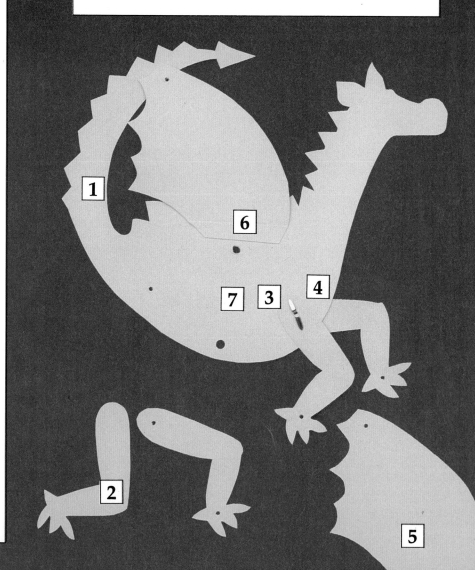

8 Join the stick to the body by pushing it through the holes you have just made in the body. You may need to use a dab of glue or some tape as well.

9 Place the middle of one piece of wire at the base of the stick. Wrap the wire around the stick twice.

10 Thread one end of the wire through the hole in one of the wings. Twist the end of the wire to make it secure. Join the other end of the wire to the other wing in the same way.

11 Wrap the second piece of wire around the stick as before. Join one end of the wire to one of the front legs and the other end to one of the back legs.

12 Wrap the third piece of wire around the stick as before. Join one end to one back leg and the other end to one front leg as you did before.

Decorate your dragon with paper shapes. To make your dragon fly, push the wire up and down the stick.

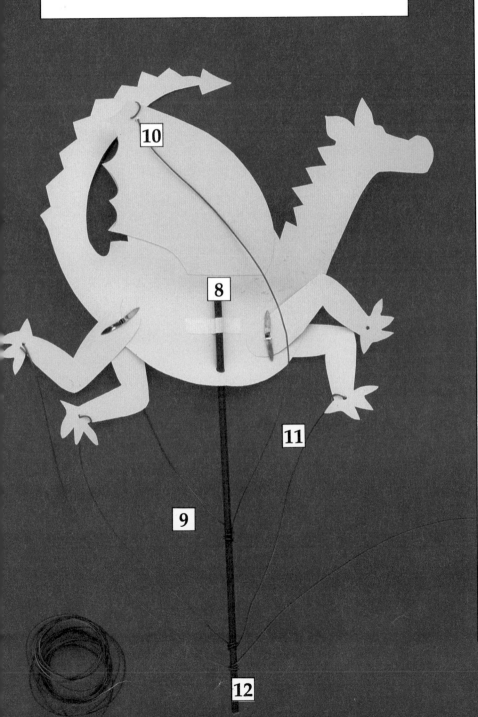

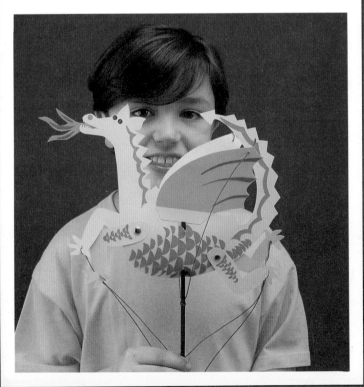

The ocean deep

"Mother-of-pearl" buttons are made from seashells. Usually, the buttons are uneven at the back and may even have shell markings. They are pearly white, and they shimmer. In the east end of London, some costermongers, people who sell fruit and vegetables from pushcarts, sew thousands of pearl buttons onto dark suits, which they wear on special occasions.

In the nineteenth century, the Trimshian, Kwakiutl, and Tlingit people of Canada decorated blankets with pearl buttons. Often, the designs on the blankets were in the shape of killer whales or other sea creatures. Similar blankets are still made today.

Try making a button blanket

You will need:	
• felt	• white glue
• plastic pearly buttons	• a needle
• sequins	• thread

Draw your creature on felt and cut it out. It's best to use a bold-colored felt, such as black, red, yellow, or blue. Glue or sew the animal shape onto a different colored piece of felt or fabric.

First, sew buttons or sequins onto the outline of the creature. Then sew buttons or sequins on for features, such as eyes. If your animal is a fish, add fins and a backbone. You can cover the creature's shape with buttons or sequins or leave it plain — whichever you think looks best. Try to make a border from buttons to frame your picture.

Try making your button blanket into a
wall hanging or a cushion.

Flying fish

May 5 is Children's Day in Japan, a national holiday. Many children hang kites in the shape of carp outside their homes. The kites can be made from paper or fabric. When the wind blows, the carp kites fill with air and look as though they are swimming in water. The carp stands for strength, energy, and long life.

Try making a carp kite to fly in the wind

You will need:
- paper or fabric
- scissors
- white glue or a needle and thread and four sewing pins
- a strip of cardboard
- a hole puncher
- a bamboo stick
- string
- felt-tip pens or fabric markers

1 Fold a piece of paper or fabric into a rectangle and draw the outline of a fish with a wide mouth. Glue the four corners of the paper together or pin the four edges of the fabric together. Cut out the shape of the fish.

2 Join the sides of the fish together with glue or close stitches. Leave both ends free for the wind to blow through.

3 Cut a thin strip of cardboard to fit around the inside of the mouth. At either side, make holes with a hole puncher, as shown. Glue and let dry.

4 Paint or draw scales and fins on your fish. Thread some string through the holes in the mouth and tie a knot further down the string. Attach the other end of the string to a stick.

Stand with your kite in the wind or tie it to a pole to make a windsock. Don't fly your kite near overhead wires.

Try making kites from other animal shapes; for example, a bird, a snake, or an octopus with eight legs that flap in the wind.

3

4

Noah and Jonah

In many parts of the world, there are stories about a great flood. Here is one from the Bible. God warned a man called Noah of the coming flood, so Noah built a huge boat called an ark for his family and two of each kind of animal. After forty days and forty nights the flood stopped, and all the animals were set free. Then the first rainbow appeared, which was God's promise to Noah that the world would never be destroyed by water again.

This painted silk picture shows a Moslem version of the story of the flood.

The story of Jonah and the whale also appears in the Bible. It tells of Jonah, who lived in the belly of a whale for three days. Find out more about this story.

A thaumatrope is a Victorian spinning toy that appears to make pictures combine. A thaumatrope that has a picture of a goldfish on one side and a picture of a bowl on the other spins to show a goldfish in a bowl. Try making some thaumatropes that put the animals inside the ark or Jonah inside the whale.

You will need:
- cardboard
- a compass or a small, round container lid
- a knitting needle
- string
- a pencil
- scissors
- white glue
- paints and paint-brushes or scraps of paper and colored pens

1 Draw two circles the same size on the cardboard. You can make the circles with a compass or by tracing the top of the container lid. Cut them out.

2 Decide which story you want to show, then paint, draw, or make a paper collage of two pictures that tell the story.

3 Glue the circles together with the pictures facing out. Make two holes 1/4 inch (5 millimeters) from the edge of the circle, as shown. Thread a piece of string through each hole and knot it tightly at the ends.

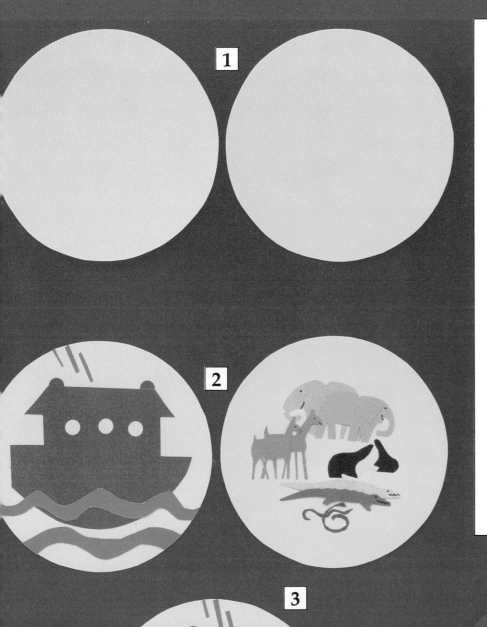

To make the thaumatrope spin, hold each end of the string and loosely flip the circle over and over itself so that the string is wound tight. Then hold the string taut and watch your pictures appear to combine.

The Haida raven

The Haida people of North America tell the story of a raven that escaped from a great flood by perching on the top of the highest mountain. As the flood ebbed, the raven felt hungry and ate thousands of shellfish. Then he rested after his large meal. Suddenly he noticed a giant clam shell, full of tiny creatures, but the raven was too full to eat them.

The raven sang sweetly to the creatures and told them stories of a beautiful world full of wonderful animals. Slowly, one by one, the creatures climbed from the shell. The raven looked after them, taught them how to hunt and fish, build canoes, and play tricks. Soon the creatures were clever and didn't need the raven to look after them any more. The creatures were people.

The pictures on Haida paintings and carvings are similar to the pieces of a jigsaw puzzle because they are made from separate shapes that fit together loosely to make one picture.

Copy the basic Haida shapes pictured here onto cardboard, cut them out, and make them into a picture. Your finished picture will look very bold if you color all the shapes using only three colors.

Try inventing your own jigsaw shapes. You can use them as templates to trace around and design your own patterns and pictures. You may also try painting your patterns on a T-shirt with fabric paint. **Before you begin, ask an adult to help you read and follow the instructions on the fabric paint.**

Origami cygnets

Origami is the Japanese art of paper folding. Try making an origami cygnet, which is a baby swan. Origami can take some practice, so if you don't get it right the first time, try again!

You will need:
- origami paper or squares of thin colored paper, approximately 7 inches (17.5 cm) square

1 Fold the paper toward you diagonally.

2 Turn the paper over so its colored side is down, if necessary.

3 Fold the top corner to meet the diagonal fold.

4 Then fold the bottom corner to meet the diagonal fold.

5 Fold the white point to the left.

Fold the paper to the left along the dotted line.

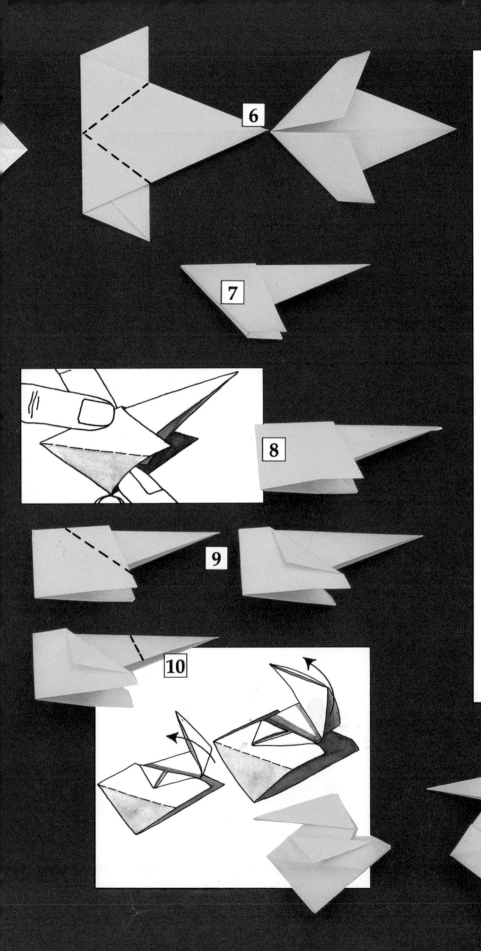

6 Turn the paper over so the point faces right.

Fold along each dotted line into the middle crease.

7 Fold the shape in half along the middle crease.

8 Pinch the top of the two wings on the middle crease and pull out the triangle of paper from underneath.

9 Make one wing tip by folding down the dotted line. Repeat on the other side to make the other wing tip.

10 Make a crease on the dotted line for the head.

To make the head, open out the point and fold the crease backward to the left.

11 To make a base for the cygnet to rest on, fold up a small triangle at the bottom.

Open the shape along the bottom fold and press the small triangle inward.

Paper peacocks

In China, paper-cutting is a traditional craft. Colored paper is cut into intricate patterns with scissors that are razor sharp. These patterns are used to make pictures. Often the paper-cut pictures are mounted on boldly colored paper so that the complicated paper cutting stands out.

Here are a few suggestions for cutting different patterns from paper that can be used to make a peacock. Try to invent your own ways of cutting paper as well.

You will need:
- colored paper
- scissors
- a pencil
- white glue

1 Cut out the shapes for the body, legs, and head feathers.

2 To make tail feathers, fold a strip of paper in half lengthwise and cut triangles from the center fold.

3 To make the "eye" parts of the tail feathers, fold a square of paper into four and cut out a quarter circle. Experiment with cutting small shapes on the folds.

4 You can make other decorations for the peacock's body by cutting three oval shapes that fit inside each other. Fold one oval in half and cut small triangles around the edges and along the center fold. Glue the ovals on top of each other, as shown.

Try creating your own animals from cut paper. Remember, it's best to cut on the fold. If you want to make your pattern more complicated, refold the paper and cut some more shapes on a different fold.

Snakes and serpents

There are stories about snakes and serpents from all over the world. In an ancient Greek story, a monster called Medusa had snakes instead of hair. Her face was so terrible that anyone who looked at her turned to stone. Eventually, a hero named Perseus cut off her head by using a mirror as a shield. He looked only at her reflection, and not at her face.

In an Aztec legend about a serpent, the Aztec gods told the Aztec people that they should settle only in the place where they found an eagle with a snake hanging from its beak. When the people saw an eagle in the middle of a lake, perched on a cactus with a snake in its beak, they built their city called Tenochtitlan. This is the same site on which Mexico City stands today.

Try making a zigzag snake

You will need:
- two toothpaste boxes that are the same size
- scissors
- colored paper and white glue or thick emulsion paints and paintbrushes

1 Cover one toothpaste box with colored paper or paint it with emulsion paint. If you cover it with paper, apply glue all over the paper first. Cover the other box with a different colored paper or paint. Cut the ends from both boxes. Flatten each box and cut into strips that are about 3/8 inch (1 cm) wide.

2 Fold one strip in half and poke its ends through the opened-out ends of a second different colored strip, as shown below.

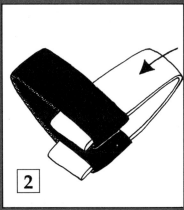

3 To make a zigzag, poke the third strip through the ends of the second strip. Continue joining the strips together until you have used all the strips.

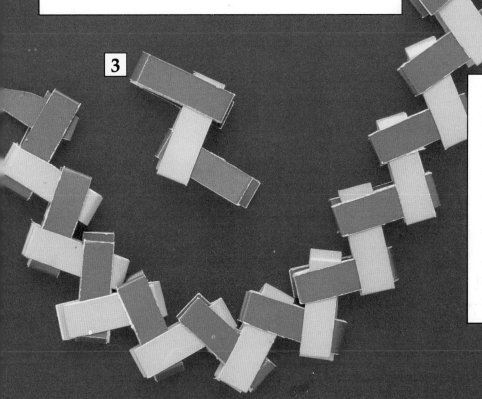

4 Cut out a cardboard head and glue it to one end of the snake. Make a tail for the other end.

What other animals can you make in this way?

Try making your snake into a puppet. Attach sticks along the back of the snake. Move the sticks to make the snake wriggle.

Lucky animals

Many animals are thought to bring good luck. In ancient Rome, in the middle of the night, a flock of geese heard the Gauls preparing to make a surprise attack. The geese made so much noise they woke the Romans up in time to defend their city. The geese became known as "watch dogs."

In parts of Pakistan, floors are decorated with lucky animal patterns, called sathia, made from dots of colored powder. Often, sathia in the shape of lucky fish and horseshoes decorate the doorsteps of people who are about to get married.

Try making a sathia decoration

You will need:
- an old shoe box lid
- paper
- colored powder paint
- a felt-tip pen
- a knitting needle
- a cork tile or old piece of carpet

1 Draw your lucky animal on the upturned box lid. Put the box lid onto a cork tile or old piece of carpet. Make holes with the knitting needle along the drawn outline, but do not make the holes too close together.

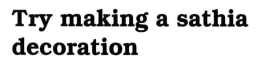

2 Put your box lid on some clean, dry concrete outside — **remember to ask permission from an adult first** — or on some paper. Use a spoon to sprinkle powder into the tray over the design. Lift the tray slightly and tap it gently at the sides. Powder should fall through the holes in the shape of your animal. If it doesn't, make the holes slightly larger and try again.

2

Horsing around

In Tamil Nadu, South India, at the entrance to some villages, there are huge models of horses made from clay. The horses are thought to bring good luck and protect the village from harm.

Make a papier-mâché horse

You will need:
- six cardboard tubes that have the same diameter and one that is slightly larger
- masking tape
- newspaper torn into strips
- a small bowl of wallpaper paste without fungicide
- paintbrushes
- paints
- scissors
- felt

1 Cut the six tubes to make pieces for four legs, a neck, and a head. Take one of the leg tubes, flatten it slightly, and cut the top at an angle so that it fits the body tube. Cut the other leg tubes in the same way. Cut the top and bottom of the neck tube and the top of the head tube at an angle as well.

2 Tape the tubes together as shown.
Cover the tubes with a layer of torn
newspaper dipped into wallpaper paste.
Cover the joints carefully. Wait for the
papier-mâché to dry. Cover the tubes
with about four layers of papier-mâché.

3 Paint your horse and decorate it
with felt. Try making your horse into
a bank by cutting a slot along its back.
Don't forget to think about how you will
get your money out.

More things to think about

This book shows you how to make and model salt dough and papier-mâché, cut and fold paper, and sew clothes for a puppet. You can use these different craft techniques to make your own items based on animals.

To get ideas for making your own crafts, think about some of the different kinds of animals in the world and the stories you know about them. Visit your local art gallery, museum, or crafts center to see how artists have shown animals now and in the past. Look for animals on pictures, statues, and signs in your city or town.

Do you believe that dragons and unicorns existed long ago? There are many stories about imaginary animals in fairy tales and ancient myths. Read some fairy tales or myths and try making a craft version of an imaginary animal.

Every country has its own customs and traditions, and some are based on animals. During Chinese New Year celebrations, people dress in large dragon costumes and dance in processions in the streets. Choose a country, such as Japan, China, India, or France, and see if you can find some traditional stories or celebrations that include animals. You can then use these ideas for your own craft projects on animals.

Think about what animals look like in real life and where different types of animals live: in water, on land, or in the air. Do you have a pet cat, dog, or fish at home? Try sketching your pet. You can look at photographs of wild animals in books and magazines, or watch nature programs on television. Look at the shape of the animal's head, body, and legs.

Does it swim, crawl, slither, or run? Keep a notebook of your findings and sketches of the animals you draw. These will be helpful when you begin your craft project.

Before you make your craft project, think about the best craft technique to use. For example, you can model salt dough or papier-mâché, or cut and fold paper. Do you want the finished model to be flat or three-dimensional? Will it have moving parts? Do you want to wear it as a mask, or will it hang somewhere? When you have answered these and other questions, think carefully about the best way of making your model and the best materials to use.

Experiment with different kinds of decoration for your craft project. You can give it spots, stripes, feathers, fur, or scales. Think about all the different ways you can create these textures with paper, cloth, or by modeling salt dough or papier-mâché. Try making a tiny lion puppet for your finger or a giant jigsaw paper cutting based on Haida shapes.

How to make salt dough

You will need:	
• 1-1/2 cups (325 grams) plain flour	• a cookie sheet
• 1 cup (250 milliliters) water	• greaseproof paper
• 1 cup (225 g) salt	• a wooden spoon
• 1 tablespoon (15 ml) oil	• a bowl
	• an oven set to 300°F (150°C)

Mix the dry ingredients together. Then add the water and oil. Shake some flour over your hands and knead the mixture into a dough.

When you have modeled the dough into the shape you want, put it on a cookie sheet lined with greaseproof paper. **Ask an adult to help you put it in the oven**. Bake for about one hour and fifteen minutes, until the model is hard.

For more information

More books to read

Adventures in Art
　Susan Milford (Williamson)

Animals Observed: A Look at Animals in Art
　Dorcas MacClintock (Charles Scribner's)

Crow and Fox and Other Animal Legends
　Jan Thornhill (Simon & Schuster)

Fun with Paint
　Moira Butterfield (Random House)

Fun with Paper Bags and Cardboard Tubes
　Virginia Walter (Sterling)

Hands Around the World
　Susan Milford (Williamson)

The Kids Multicultural Art Book
　Alexandra M. Terzian (Williamson)

Magical Tales from Many Lands
　Margaret Mayo (Dutton)

Making Presents
　Juliet Bawden (Random House)

My First Activity Book
　Angela Wilkes (Knopf)

My First Nature Craft Book
　Cheryl Owen (Little, Brown, and Co.)

Papier-Mâché for Kids
　Sheila McGraw (Firefly Books)

60 Art Projects for Children
　Jeannette M. Baumgardner
　(Clarkson Potter)

Stories in Art
　Helen Williams (Millbrook Press)

Videos

Aesop's Fables (Western Publishing)

Don't Eat the Pictures
　(Children's Television Workshop)

How the Kiwi Lost His Wings
　(Churchill Films)

Look What I Made: Paper Playthings and Gifts

My First Activity Video (Sony)

Places to visit

The following places have major collections of crafts from around the world. Don't forget to look in your area museum, too.

Canadian Museum of Civilization
100 Laurier Street
P.O. Box 3100, Station B
Hull, Quebec
J8X 4H2

Denver Museum of Natural History
2001 Colorado Boulevard
Denver, Colorado 80205

Franklin Institute
20th Street and the Franklin Parkway
Philadelphia, Pennsylvania 19103-1194

Royal British Columbia Museum
675 Belleville Street
Victoria, British Columbia
V8V 1X4

The Smithsonian Institution
1000 Jefferson Drive SW
Washington, D.C. 20560

Index

For a free color catalog describing Gareth Stevens' list of high-quality books, call 1-800-542-2595 (USA) or 1-800-461-9120 (Canada). Gareth Stevens' Fax: (414) 225-0377.

Library of Congress Cataloging-in-Publication Data
MacLeod-Brudenell, Iain.
    Animal crafts/Iain MacLeod-Brudenell; photographs by Zul Mukhida.
    North American ed.
        p. cm. — (Worldwide crafts)
    Includes bibliographical references and index.
    ISBN 0-8368-1151-8
    1. Handicraft—Juvenile literature. 2. Paper work—Juvenile literature. 3. Animals in art—Juvenile literature. 4. Animals, Mythical, in art—Juvenile literature. [1. Handicraft. 2. Paper work. 3. Animals in art. 4. Animals, Mythical, in art.] I. Mukhida, Zul, ill. II. Title. III. Series.
    TT160.M2584   1994
    745.5—dc20   94-11434

North American edition first published in 1994 by
Gareth Stevens Publishing
1555 North RiverCenter Drive, Suite 201
Milwaukee, Wisconsin 53212, USA

First published in 1993 by A & C Black (Publishers) Limited, London; © 1993 A & C Black (Publishers) Limited.

Acknowledgments
Line drawings by Barbara Pegg. Photographs by Zul Mukhida, except for pages 14 and 16 Life File Photographic Agency.

Grateful thanks to Langford and Hill, Ltd., London, for supplying all art materials.

Crafts made by Dorothy Moir except for those on pp. 4-5, 6-7, 8-9, 28-29, which were made by Tracy Brunt.